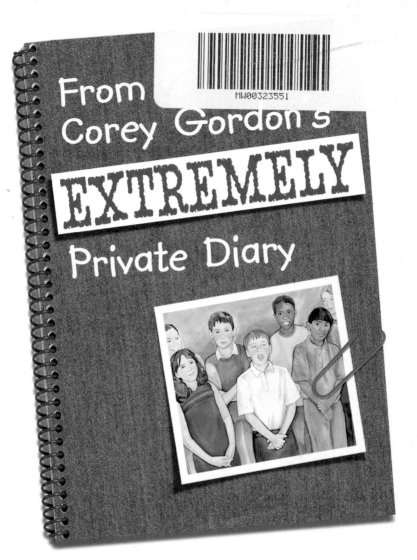

From Corey Gordon's EXTREMELY Private Diary

By Lynn Cullen
Illustrated by Jan Naimo Jones

Celebration Press
Pearson Learning Group

CONTENTS

Chapter 1

If you are reading this now, YOU ARE SNOOPING IN PRIVATE PROPERTY. If you know what's good for you, YOU WILL CLOSE THIS BOOK IMMEDIATELY. The penalty for snooping will be swift and terrible!

Corey C. Gordon
Commonly known as
Corey the Great

Keeping a diary wasn't my idea. What if you write down something really important and somebody reads it? But I'm stuck. Mrs. Knight is making us keep one for our English class for this whole month. She said we're to bring it to class so she can check to see if we've used it every day. She promised she wouldn't read a word of it. She just wants us to get used to writing about our feelings.

Well, I don't want to write about my feelings. I want to organize my baseball cards in the new album I got for my birthday last week. You won't catch me putting down stuff that's really personal.

Tuesday, April 2

Dear Diary,

I don't have anything to say, especially
to an empty book, so I'm not going to say
anything. I guess I'm in trouble now, aren't I,
Mrs. Knight?

Wednesday, April 3

I was waiting for Mrs. Knight to yell at me
for what I wrote yesterday (or didn't write).
But when she came around to my desk, all
she did was look at the page, then put a little
check in her grade book. Maybe I really can
say anything I want to. Okay, then I will.

I AM SICK OF BEING THE SHORTEST BOY
IN THE FIFTH GRADE.

It's true. I'm tired of the girls thinking I'm cute.
Puppies are cute. Kittens are cute. Fifth-grade
boys are not cute!

And I'm fed up with the guys making fun of me.
Whenever we pass the kindergarten table at
lunchtime, Ross Spellman always says, "Hey

Corey, there's your class." It wasn't funny the first time. You'd think that at least he'd come up with something new to say. I wish just once Ross Spellman would throw a net-nicker when we play basketball in P.E. I wish that just one time Mrs. Knight would ask him to get down on his knees and crawl into her bottom cupboard and pull out art supplies. Why can't all the room mothers say he's "cute" and I'm "handsome," just once? (My ears might be small, but they're sharp.)

Since Mrs. Knight isn't reading this, and won't be able to think I'm jealous or anything ridiculous like that, I have one more thing I would like to say.

I CAN'T STAND MY LITTLE BROTHER!!!

My brother Walker is two years old. He has tantrums, scribbles on walls, and wears his breakfast on a daily basis, yet people love him. They think it's hilarious when he pouts and says no when he really means yes. They chuckle when he takes the blank labels out of my baseball-card album and sticks them all over himself. They say, "Look at his darling red curls," which are exactly like mine, though nobody comments on my darling hair. But I wouldn't want them to. I don't spend ten minutes every morning flattening mine with water and gel for nothing.

I wish just one person would say, "Yes, I see the boring little kid over there, but would you look at his amazing big brother!" I'd even take being called adorable, just as long as I was the one being noticed, not him. Who thought I'd ever want to be called adorable?

Life was good until Walker came along. I had my mom and dad all to myself. I was the center of their attention for nine whole years. They were always there for me. But the minute Walker was born, everything changed. All of a sudden the entire house revolved around this noisy, extremely needy creature that looked like a tiny old man with a sunburn. That's when I got into baseball cards. They're always there waiting for me, unlike parents with babies.

This was a bad day. I might be stuck singing a solo for the spring music program. I can't do it! Really, I can't! HELP!

This is how it happened. For weeks we've been practicing the songs we're going to sing for the spring music program next Tuesday night. I've sung them so much they go around and around in my head all day.

Not that the songs excite me. I'm not much of a musician. This boy in my class, Ramon Martinez, is the kid who can really sing. He has a solo in one of the songs. Whenever he sings it, we have to stand still on the risers and be quiet.

That's okay by me. I use the time to imagine what it would be like to be two feet taller. I picture myself slam-dunking baskets in P.E. Or getting things out of the top cabinet for Mrs. Knight. Or patting Ross Spellman on the head like a good little boy.

But today I was just getting into Dream Mode when the music stopped. Ramon was over by the

8

music teacher, Mrs. Bartlett, pointing at his throat. She started playing the piano again, but all that came out of Ramon's mouth was a funny squawk. He said his throat hurt.

Mrs. Bartlett felt his forehead. "You're burning up," she said, and sent him straight to the office.

"Who will take Ramon's place?" Mrs. Bartlett asked. She paced in front of the risers, but I was looking at Ross, wondering if I would ever be his size. Then I heard Mrs. Bartlett's voice. "Corey."

I thought she was going to yell at me for daydreaming. "Sorry, Mrs. Bartlett," I said. "I couldn't hear what you said."

She frowned. "That is probably because I didn't say anything." She raised her thick eyebrows, which always remind me of two furry little animals. "How would you feel about singing Ramon's solo?"

Sing a solo for the spring music program! Every drop of blood must have left my head, making my face completely pale. I thought I was going to slither down between the risers. I guess I must have looked sort of weird because the nicest girl in the class, Lucy Tucker, gasped. "What?" I croaked.

"You have such a beautiful voice," Mrs. Bartlett said. "If Ramon can't sing Tuesday, I'd like you to take the solo. Would you like to give it a try?"

I looked around wildly. Everyone was watching me. If I said no, I would look like a cowardly chicken. If I said yes, with my awful voice I would sound like a chicken—squawk, squawk. I could never sing a solo in front of an audience.

I told her I didn't know the part very well.

"Surely you must," she said. "We've been practicing for two months. What have you been doing when Ramon's been singing?"

All the blood that had rushed from my head came pouring back. They'd laugh me out of the room if they knew how I'd been using the time. Suddenly it was as if they could see my daydreams.

I couldn't speak.

"Aw," said Ross Spellman, "he's just afraid. Want me to do it, Mrs. Bartlett?"

Everybody turned away from me and toward Ross. I know I wasn't imagining it—Lucy Tucker was gaping at him as if he had just saved the world. Other girls were, too.

Suddenly I had the same terrible feeling I had the day Walker came home from the hospital. There's one thing worse than being embarrassed— it's being ignored.

Mrs. Bartlett walked back over to the piano and sat down. "Ross, if you want to give it a try—"

"No!" I shouted. "I'll do it."

Mrs. Bartlett's twin furry creatures arched their backs on her forehead.

"Really," I said. I stood up straight, just as tall as I could. Then I told the biggest fib of my life. "It'll be easy."

Mrs. Bartlett nodded and handed me Ramon's music. "All right, Corey," she said. "Let's try it." My heart thumped in my ears louder than Walker banging on a pot. I could almost feel my legs running me out of the room.

At that very moment the shrill sound of the fire alarm came blaring from the hall. Everyone started talking and climbing down off the risers.

"Fire drill!" said Mrs. Bartlett. "Quickly, everyone in single file to the playground!"

I ran to be the first in line. I led my class outside as if the school really were on fire. We spent the rest of the period outside on the playground. Talk about being saved by the bell! I loved that fire drill so much I could have gone out in the hall and kissed the buzzer. I guess miracles can happen. The problem is, unless Ramon gets well, I need another miracle—fast.

Chapter 2

Saturday, April 6

I had a horrible dream just before I woke up this morning. I was on the risers, and a crowd of kids and parents and grandparents were sitting in the audience. Their eyes were all aimed in my direction. Their stares were hammering me like a thousand dodgeballs. Then my turn came to sing Ramon's song. I opened my mouth, but nothing came out. I just stood there with my mouth open, like a dead fish, not making a sound. What did I get myself into?

The dream seemed so real. I couldn't sing, or even speak. At first just the grandparents in the audience chuckled. Then the parents chimed in. Then the kids took over, giggling at first, then guffawing out loud.

As they jeered and hooted, I started shrinking. First I was the size of a kindergarten kid. Then I shrank to the size of Walker. When I was finished shrinking, I was no bigger than a cringing little mouse.

I had almost disappeared from the risers when Walker woke me up. "I 'ticker." He was putting the labels for my baseball-card album on the front of his shirt. "I 'ticker," he said again.

I sat up. "You may want a sticker, but those aren't yours. They aren't even stickers. They're labels." I hopped out of bed and ripped one of the blank labels off his shirt. "Get out."

A huge frown took over Walker's face. He yelled so loud you would have thought he had just gotten his hand slammed in the door. Mom came tearing in. "What's wrong?"

"Get him out!" I said. "He's in my labels again." Mom laughed. *Laughed.* "He's been a sticker maniac ever since they gave him one at the doctor's office. He's been on the lookout for anything with glue on the back. Yesterday he got into my postage stamps."

"Well," I said, "these are not stickers, and they happen to be private property."

Mom took a label from Walker's chest and put it back on its paper. "You're right. Walker shouldn't be allowed to get into your things without your permission. But would it be so hard for you to play with him now and then? It would make him so happy, Corey. You're his big brother. He loves you so much."

I told her that the feeling was not mutual. What I didn't tell her was that I don't happen to like him at all. Why does she always have to take his side? She sticks up for him even when he's bad. She would have yelled at me if I'd wasted her stamps. I could just hear her yelling, "Postage costs money!" Does she have to make it so obvious that he is her favorite kid?

The day didn't get any better. Thinking about my solo, I could hardly eat breakfast. I could barely watch Saturday morning television. I couldn't even look at my baseball cards. Why did I say I would do it? I should have let Ross take the solo. Let him make a fool of himself!

I decided that I'd better practice. Then Walker kept coming into my room to listen, so I locked myself in the bathroom. The shower was the only place I could get away from the little pest. I practiced until I turned the bathroom into a fog. I built up so much steam it was like being in my own soapy-smelling cloud.

Actually I almost got to like the song. I decided that maybe I didn't sound too terrible. But singing in the shower is different from singing in front of hundreds of people. What if I miss a word or hit a wrong note? Everyone will laugh. How am I going to do this?

At dinner I asked my dad to tell me how he handles speaking to large groups of people. I figured that speaking in front of a lot of people was almost as bad as singing a solo to them. Anytime an audience gets to stare at you is bad news. Anyway, Dad's the principal of a high school, and he has to talk in public a lot. You wouldn't believe how many banquets and sporting events and teachers' meetings principals have to speak at.

"Speaking to groups doesn't bother me anymore," he said. "I've done it so much I'm used to it."

That didn't help me. "I'll never get used to performing in front of people," I said.

Dad grinned. "One thing I've learned in life," he said, "is to 'never say never.' "

That didn't make sense. It didn't help me in my time of need either. "What about before you were used to it?" I asked.

Dad salted his chicken. "I just practiced my material a lot before I spoke. If I was familiar with what I was doing, I had more confidence."

I pushed around my mashed potatoes with my fork. I didn't feel a bit hungry. I had practiced my song over and over again in the shower until my skin puckered. I couldn't know that tune any better than I already did.

But knowing that solo perfectly didn't help solve what bothered me the most. How could I ever let people hear my singing voice? What if the audience thought I sounded weird?

"What if you had to sing in front of people?" I asked Dad. "Wouldn't you be afraid of sounding strange?"

My dad shrugged. "I'd just do my best." Then he went back to eating his dinner.

18

"But what if you made a mistake right in the middle of your song?" I asked. "What if people laughed?"

Dad smiled and cut into his chicken. "I'd laugh with them."

I gaped at my dad. He can't be human.

Just then Walker smeared a handful of mashed potatoes in his hair.

Mom jumped up. "Oh, Walker! Bad!"

Walker grinned as a glob of mashed potato slid from his ear onto his plate.

"That is not funny," Mom said, wiping the side of his head with her napkin. "If you don't eat your potatoes, you don't get cookies for dessert. Don't you want a cookie?"

"No," said Walker. "No cookie."

I shook my head. Walker likes eating cookies more than anything. I think he likes them even more than getting into my baseball cards.

"Well," said Mom, "I'm glad that you don't want a cookie, because if you put food in your hair, you're much too much of a baby to have cookies."

Walker yelled, "I not baby! I not baby!" He arched his back, climbed down from his booster seat, then wriggled snakelike under the table, and fell to the floor. Before my mother could catch him, he got up and scuttled into the family room.

From my seat at the table, I watched as Walker threw himself into Dad's favorite chair. Turning around to sit in it, he bumped into the lamp on the table beside it. It was my mom's special lamp, given to her by her grandmother. Now it was rocking back and forth like a boat in choppy water.

"Walker!" Mom cried out. She raced over and grabbed the lamp right before it fell.

"Safe!" Dad said. Then he took another bite of chicken.

Mom gasped. She looked at the lamp, then at Dad, then she burst out laughing. After a minute she returned the lamp to its place.

I wondered if Mom would have laughed if I had been the one who almost broke her lamp. Then I excused myself from the table. Between my crazy family and the thought of my upcoming solo, my dinner was ruined.

Please, please, please, let Ramon get well.

Chapter 3

Sunday, April 7

I thought over Dad's advice. I can't see myself joining in as the audience laughs at my expense. I think I would rather recite the Gettysburg Address in a tutu. I guess the best I can do is to practice a lot. If I don't make a mistake, kids can only laugh at how dumb my voice is.

That thought alone makes me sick to my stomach.

Ramon, you've got to get well.

I practiced singing my solo in my room most of that Sunday afternoon. After I'd been at it for what seemed like hours, I decided to test out my voice on Mom.

She was in the kitchen with Walker. There was a huge sheet of paper on the floor, with Walker sitting in the middle of it. He was smearing globs of paint onto the paper and smiling happily and talking to himself.

"What's he doing now?" I asked.

"Painting," said Mom. "Better on paper with his fingers than all over the walls with a crayon."

I couldn't remember Mom ever finger painting with me. It was obvious who her favorite child was. I would have walked away right then, but I was too desperate. "Mom," I said, "if Ramon is not back in school by Tuesday, I have to sing a solo at the spring music program."

"Oh, Corey," Mom said, "that's great!"

"No, it's not," I said. "Everyone is going to laugh at me."

"Now, why would they do that?" she said. "You have a really beautiful voice."

A weak ray of hope flickered in my gut. "Do you think so?"

"Of course. You've always sung well."

I suddenly felt much more confident. "Will you listen to me sing my part and then tell me what I should change?"

I sang her my solo. It felt weird belting it out in the kitchen. When I was done, Walker was looking up at me, sucking his thumb, a ring of dark blue paint around his mouth.

"Corey, that was great," Mom said. "Your voice is just beautiful. I am going to be so proud."

I ducked my head, embarrassed in front of my own mother. I wished she'd said my voice sounded "manly" or "awesome," but "beautiful" was pretty good, I guess. It was definitely better than "horrible."

Just then Mom said, "Oh, look, Walker! Is that a doggy you made?"

I looked at Walker. On the paper in front of him was a blue blob with three smeary legs.

Walker nodded. "Daw doggy."

"Yes, Walker," said Mom, "you did draw a doggy! You are such an artist. Both my boys are so talented."

Walker beamed.

25

I turned around and marched to my room. "Corey!" Mom called after me. "Come back. I loved your song!"

Sure she did—as much as she loved Walker's blue blob. I saw how bad his artwork was. He had no talent whatsoever. A chimp with a toothbrush could do better. Mom was just being nice—she likes everything. I could be terrible, and she'd never tell me.

Or maybe she just loves everything Walker does, no matter how crummy it is. She doesn't even bother to hide how much more she likes him than me. Even if I had sung okay, she wouldn't have noticed. She was too busy going nuts over Walker's chimp art.

Now I had no idea if my voice was good. For all I knew, I sounded like a wounded elephant—with a head cold. The minute I opened my mouth, kids were going to fall down laughing from the risers. They would never forget the night Corey Gordon made an absolute fool of himself. I would forever be the short kid with the rotten voice.

Chapter 4

Monday, April 8

This was a bad, bad, bad, bad day.

At first, everything was going my way. Good old Ramon was back in school. Lucy Tucker was paying attention to me, not to Ross Spellman.

Then, just when I thought everything was going to be okay, I tripped on my shoelace right in front of Lucy, and Ramon got sick again and had to go home. Now what am I going to do? The program is tomorrow night, and I can't get out of it! Where are miracles when you need them?

Help!

I am in huge, huge trouble.

It's amazing how fast a good day can go bad. In the morning before school today, I happened to see Ramon in the cafeteria. The minute I laid eyes on him, I wanted to run over and hug him. He'd saved my life! When I waved at him instead, he frowned and looked over his shoulder.

I think he thought I was being weird. I didn't care because I was in a great mood.

I didn't even mind when Mrs. Knight asked me to get her pencil when it rolled under the corner table. I didn't come out from underneath the table as quickly as usual. Instead I curled up and pretend-snored until Mrs. Knight called me in an exasperated voice and made me move. A lot of kids laughed—especially Lucy Tucker. Whenever she laughs, the corners of her eyes crinkle up. I like that.

Later, we went to the gym and practiced for the music program. Ramon sang great. Well, his voice was a little hoarse, but he sounded better than I would have.

Then, just before it was time to catch the bus at the end of the day, Mrs. Bartlett hurried into our room and called me out into the hall. I knew it couldn't be good news.

"Corey," she said, "Ramon just went home. He has a fever of 102. His mother said she let him come to school today because he claimed he was well, but obviously he's not."

I think I must have groaned.

"Are you sick, too?" asked Mrs. Bartlett.

At that moment it wouldn't have been a lie to say that I was sick. I felt so rotten I couldn't open my mouth. But I shook my head no.

"Good," said Mrs. Bartlett. "I'm glad you're well. Ramon's mother is taking him to the doctor. I think we need to plan on your singing the solo tomorrow."

The bell rang and kids started pouring out of their rooms. That didn't stop Mrs. Bartlett.

"I know you didn't get to practice with the chorus," she said. "I'm sorry, Corey, because that makes it all the harder for you. Do you think you can handle this?"

Just then Ross Spellman walked up. Lucy Tucker was right behind him. "Is he backing out on you, Mrs. Bartlett?" Ross asked.

Lucy Tucker was watching.

I threw back my shoulders, though it made my already sick stomach lurch. "I'm not backing out on anything," I said.

"Corey," said Mrs. Bartlett, "you really are a lifesaver."

Lucy Tucker smiled and then she ran to her bus. Oh, why couldn't this "lifesaver" have a fever of 102 like Ramon?

At home I went back to nonstop practicing.

Just before dinner Dad leaned into my room as I was hitting the highest note.

"Sounds good, Corey," he said.

I nodded. I didn't know if I could believe him any more than I could believe Mom.

"Your mother has cut her finger on the lid of a tomato sauce can," he said, "and I think she needs to have stitches. We're going to the emergency room now. Could you please watch Walker until we get back? Mrs. Gomez next door says she will be home if you need her."

"But Dad," I said, "I have to practice my solo. You said yourself, you have to know your material."

"That's right," said Dad, "but this is an emergency. You can practice your solo while you're watching Walker."

"Robert," Mom called, "I'm ready to go."

"Just keep practicing," said Dad. "Don't worry, Walker shouldn't be too much trouble."

It was awful. I didn't get one note of practicing in. Walker was full of energy. When I gave him dinner, he smeared applesauce all over his overalls. When I was cleaning up the mess he'd made at the table, he carved a "doggy" in the kitchen doorframe with Dad's pen.

When I was trying to erase the pen marks, he chewed on one of my baseball cards. It was one of my favorites, a Cal Ripken, Jr. I smoothed out the edges, but I could still see tooth marks.

Then Walker wouldn't go to sleep, even after I read four of his favorite books to him.

Finally, I'd had it. "Stay awake," I said in a cross voice. "See if I care, but when you're tired and grumpy tomorrow, don't blame me."

Walker leaned over and picked up one of the books I'd already read. "Read," he said, trying to give me the book.

"Walker," I said, "you just don't get it, do you?"

I went out into the family room and plopped down in Dad's chair. It took me a while to clear my head enough to be able to practice my part. But just as I started, Walker came toddling out of his bedroom and made for the chair.

"Me scared," he said.

I kept on singing. Maybe if I ignored him he'd go away. But Walker didn't go away.

"Me scared," he said again.

I wasn't giving in to the spoiled baby. I sang on, trying to be ready for the big night.

"Me sit, Corey," he said. He tottered over and with determination started hauling himself up into the chair beside me.

"Go to bed," I said, but he didn't stop. He was wiggling up next to me when his foot accidentally bumped Mom's special lamp, which began rocking back and forth.

I reached, but not fast enough. The lamp tipped over like a bowling pin and then landed with a crash. What had been a pretty blue jar was now a pile of glass topped with a lampshade.

Walker blinked at the mess. "Uh-oh."

"We are in deep trouble," I said. "We are in deep, deep trouble."

I looked at Walker. There was still a trace of blue around his mouth from when he'd been painting yesterday. "We trouble," he whispered.

Then it occurred to me. "Wait a minute," I said. "We aren't in trouble. I'm not the one who smeared applesauce all over your overalls. I'm not the one who carved doggies on the wall, and especially, I'm not the one who broke this lamp. You are."

Walker stared at the pile of lamp bits. "Me broke," he whimpered.

Suddenly I was glad. When Mom came home, she would see Walker for what he was—a monster. A wall-scribbling, paint-eating, lamp-breaking monster! Then she would know who her best kid was—me.

Just then car doors slammed and the door from the garage opened. Mom walked into the room. Then she screamed, "Grandma's lamp!" She dropped to her knees next to the remains.

"Oh, Carol, I'm so sorry," said Dad. "I'll get a broom and dustpan."

Her reaction was everything I had hoped for. I was quick to explain. "Walker did it," I said. "He's been wild all night."

Walker's lower lip inched forward. "I bad."

I snorted, "You sure are!" I looked up at Mom and Dad, waiting for the explosion I'd craved ever since Walker had come home from the hospital.

Mom leaned forward on her knees. I thought she was going to gather together the broken pieces of the lamp, but instead she reached out for Walker. He toddled toward her and she picked him up.

He burst into tears. Mom cradled him in her arms. "Shh, now," she said. She rocked him back and forth. "It's okay."

"Okay?" I yelled. "He broke your lamp! Aren't you even going to punish him?"

Mom rested her cheek on Walker's head. "I think he's already sorry."

"But it was your special lamp!" I said. "You can't just let him get away with it."

Mom looked at me over Walker's curls. "Did I ever tell you that this lamp was one of a pair?"

After all I'd been through with Walker, I wasn't in the mood for stories. "No," I replied.

"Grandma gave me two identical lamps," Mom said. "But its mate was broken nine years ago, when you were two."

"How?" I asked, not really interested in hearing the answer.

"By you," explained Mom.

Now I was really feeling crabby. "I don't remember breaking any lamp."

Mom smiled. "You wouldn't. It was an accident. You were getting a book for me to read. Unfortunately the books were next to the lamp."

I didn't like the way this story seemed to be going. "Oh," I said.

"When you knocked it over, you were just as upset at Walker is now. I comforted you and tried not to make a big deal of it. I figured your feelings were much more important than a lamp."

I frowned at the lamp pieces on the floor. Had I really broken one, too? I couldn't see myself as a two-year-old, tearing around the house, ruining people's property. "I was never like Walker," I said.

Dad was back with the broom. "Everybody was two years old once, Corey," he said. "Thank goodness, they finally grow up." He started sweeping the broken pieces into the dustpan.

I went to my room. I could never have been as goofy, messy, and annoying as Walker is.

Could I?

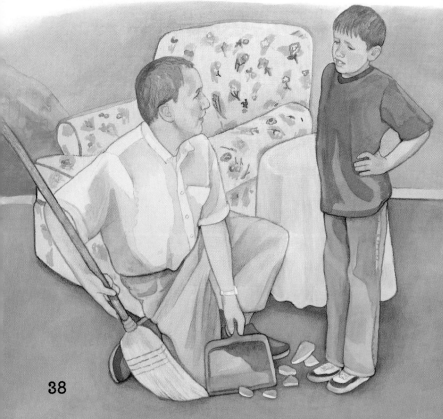

Chapter 5

Tuesday, April 9

What a crazy day it's been. First, the minute I got to school, I went to Ramon's homeroom to find out for sure if he was still sick. When he didn't show up by the first bell, I knew he wasn't coming. After that, I couldn't even think. All during my first class, I was in a fog. People talked to me, and I didn't hear them. I bumped into kids without seeing them. I was so absentminded at lunch that I actually got in the trash line with the kindergarten kids. But somehow tonight I sang and I survived.

I still can't believe it. Maybe miracles do happen. Or maybe you can make them happen, if you try hard enough.

Ross thought it was really hilarious when I lined up with the kindergarten kids. "You finally found your class, Corey!" he yelled. He made sure that everybody in the cafeteria saw me, especially Lucy. She looked embarrassed for me. That's worse than actually feeling embarrassed yourself.

Later Mrs. Knight asked me to crawl under the corner table to get a box of art supplies she had stored there. Singing my part in my head, I kind of forgot what I was doing. I just sat there under the table, holding the box, the melody to my solo going through my brain.

Mrs. Knight leaned over to look at me. "Corey? You didn't fall asleep again, did you?"

She surprised me so much I jerked and hit the table with my head. I tried to cover for it by acting like I meant to do it, but nobody bought it.

"No, ma'am, I didn't," I answered.

Everybody in English class laughed, except for Lucy. She just looked ashamed for me.

I figured they were just warming up for tonight. When I stood in front of the whole school, there would be no covering up my bad singing, and the laughter would be heard for miles.

As awful as the day was, it went fast. Before I knew it, dinner was over, and I was dressed in my white shirt and navy pants, ready to go and sing. I trudged out to the kitchen. I felt as if I were going to the dentist to have all my teeth pulled.

Mom said I looked great.

Uh-huh. Just like Walker did last night, with that crust of applesauce in his hair.

Dad came in with the car keys. "Are you ready to sing?" he asked.

"I'll never be ready."

Dad winked. "Never say never."

I didn't know what he meant by that, but I just wished he'd never say it again.

My parents drove me to school. I sat in the back seat, my stomach all knotted up.

"I can't do this," I told them. "I'm too nervous. I'll make a mistake. Take me home."

"You have to get your mind off of it, Corey," said Dad. "Think of something else, something that requires complete concentration."

I took a deep breath and tried to think of my baseball cards. I pictured my Reggie Jackson, my Sammy Sosa, my Mike Piazza.

Then I imagined my chewed-up Cal Ripken, Jr., and lost my concentration. All I could think about was making a mistake with my solo.

The next thing I knew, I was on the risers. The audience was buzzing before me, and the music was ready to start.

We sang the first two songs—that is, everyone else sang. I couldn't open my mouth. My hands were cold and wet. My head pounded. I remembered what Dad said about getting my mind on something else. CONCENTRATE, I told myself, CONCENTRATE. But I couldn't. All I could think of was failure.

The second song ended and the audience clapped. Then Mrs. Bartlett bent over the piano. The crowd hushed as the first few notes of the next song floated over them. It was "the big one." I took a deep breath. In a few short minutes, I was going to become the laughingstock of the school.

At that very moment, a small voice rang out over the music. "Corey song!"

Walker stood up on Mom's lap. He clapped his hands. "Corey song!" he crowed again.

I wanted to crawl under the risers. Crazy two-year-old brother!

Mrs. Bartlett kept playing as if Walker weren't making a scene. The rest of the chorus kept singing along with her as Walker clapped and shouted. How could the people in the audience think he was funny? The more they laughed, the more he yelled, "Corey!" The whole audience was acting like a bunch of two-year-olds. I was never going to be able to concentrate enough to sing my solo now.

Then, as I ran my wet hands through my hair, my stomach twisting in knots, Dad's words came back to me, "Everybody was two years old once. Thank goodness, they finally grow up."

I looked up as the chorus got nearer to my part, my mouth dropping open. What if I pictured every single person in that gym as a two-year-old? Could I then get over my nerves enough to sing my song?

I made myself focus on the first person I saw. It was a white-haired lady in the first row, wearing a bright green dress. I forced myself to picture her as a two-year-old. I made the wrinkles disappear from her face and replaced them with the ornery look of a toddler. I imagined her white hair as blond curls—blond curls crusty with the applesauce she'd smeared on them.

Grinning to myself, I turned to the dad standing in the aisle, recording us with his video camera. Using my new trick, I imagined his suit as a pair of baby overalls, then pictured him holding a fat crayon instead of a camera. I made myself see him take that crayon and scribble on his kitchen wall.

Still smiling from that, I looked at my own mom, now struggling to get Walker to sit down. I saw her as I'd seen her in her baby pictures, with long blond hair and a happy look in her eyes. I imagined her running around her house as a two-year-old, laughing as she was being chased by my uncle Bill. I saw her dodge to get out of his reach. Maybe she'd even broken a lamp herself at some time and cried. Grandma would have picked her up and comforted her.

Then an elbow nudged my rib. It was Mark, the kid standing next to me. "Now," he whispered. I recognized the first two notes of my solo coming from the piano. Mrs. Bartlett was staring at me in alarm. I jumped right into my song, too surprised to be afraid.

I'm not sure, but I think I did okay. At least the crowd was quiet—with no laughing—until I was done.

Then Walker crowed, "My brudder!" and everyone clapped very loudly.

What a relief to have it over with! When the rest of the chorus joined in after my solo, I sang with them like some kind of opera singer. I felt great!

But even as I sang, I realized that I couldn't turn off my brain. Once I'd gotten started, I kept seeing everybody as two-year-olds. I just couldn't stop myself.

I saw Mrs. Bartlett as a toddler in pigtails, stomping her foot and saying no when she really meant yes.

I pictured Ross eating finger paint and then grinning with a blue mouth.

Then I imagined Lucy as a toddler. She was eating a baseball card, looking guilty. She left cute little tooth marks around the edges.

As I stood there, singing at the top of my lungs, I was suddenly so happy I felt like I could burst. Dad was right. We were all two-year-olds once, and thank goodness we finally grew up.

As the music came to its end, and the crowd cheered and clapped and got to their feet, I said another silent thanks. Thank goodness we keep growing up all the time.

Today started out badly, but it ended up being an amazing day. I survived my solo! I never thought it was possible!

So the concert is behind me now. I guess Dad was right. By getting my mind off my fear, I was able to get the job done. But next time I have to perform, I may not think of two-year-olds. It was too hard forgetting them once I started.

I can't say that I loved doing the solo, but I did kind of like all the people congratulating me afterward. I'm not sure if I'll ever sing in front of people again, but as Dad says, "Never say never."

By the way, Lucy gave me her school picture today. I don't know what to do with it. I guess I'll keep it in my diary so I can look at it everyday.

Walker's in the other room and he's being too quiet. Maybe he has one of my baseball cards. I'd better go get him. I found some old stickers he's going to really like.